The World
According to

KALEY

by
Dian Curtis Regan

This edition is published by special arrangement with Darby Creek Publishing, 7858 Industrial Parkway, Plain City, OH 43064.

Grateful acknowledgment is made to Darby Creek Publishing, 7358 Industrial Parkway, Plain City, OH, 43064, for permission to reprint *The World According to Kaley* by Dian Curtis Regan. Text copyright © 2005 by Dian Curtis Regan; cover copyright © 2005 by Darby Creek Publishing.

Printed in the United States of America

ISBN 10 0-15-365151-2
ISBN 13 978-0-15-365151-9

1 2 3 4 5 6 7 8 9 10   947 17 16 14 13 12 11 10 09 08 07

THIS NOTEBOOK
BELONGS TO
KALEY BLUSTER

chicks rule!

World History
Grade 4
Mr. Serrano

September 18
World History
Unit: Writing Essays
Grade 4
Mr. Serrano

Assignment #1:
Discuss the early years of civilization.

People: The Early Years
by Kaley Bluster

Long ago, way before my parents were born, when my great-great-grandparents were tiny babies, dinosaurs ruled the earth.

This time in history was called the Ice Age. It was very cold and snowy in those days, but they never canceled school.

The ice smushed the dinosaurs, which is why you do not see them today. It didn't smush my baby grandparents or I wouldn't be writing this.

People who lived during the Ice Age were very messy. Even messier than my cousin, Cal, who comes over to play, then leaves balls and bats and bikes in the yard, which I have to pick up.

Ice Age people left tools and jewelry and pots lying everywhere. Plus, they drew all over their caves. This is how we learned about them. Once, I drew on the walls of my bedroom with crayons. My mom said she was not interested in "learning about me in that way."

The next age was called the Stone Age. It got its name because people made stuff out of rocks. Rock chairs, rock cars, rock TVs. It was during this era that rock-and-roll began. Today, you can still hear people mention "rock guitar."

During the Stone Age, people also discovered fire. In those days, it was okay to play with matches. Today, it is not. Just ask Cal about that mishap in our basement. Fake Christmas trees do <u>too</u> burn like real trees.

People in the Stone Age were nomads. They moved all the time, which must have been a pain for the kids who had to keep changing schools. I know because I had to change schools in 3rd grade. (Thank you, Dad.)

Nomads moved a lot because they had to follow their food supply: mammoths. Mammoths were easy to follow because they were shaggy and smelly. (Dad said we had to move to follow our money supply. I think he was trying to be funny.)

During the Stone Age, people were called hunters and gatherers. Many wars broke out, mostly over who was going to hunt and who was going to gather. It was awful.

When they grew tired of fighting, they decided once and for all by drawing straws. This is where the expression "the final straw" comes from. This is one of my Aunt Phoebe's favorite expressions. If you knew Cal, you would understand why.

About this time in history, people figured it would be a lot easier to argue if they invented a language. Once they began to understand what all the grunts and groans meant, there was no stopping them.

After that, it was only a matter of time before cell phones were invented so people could talk anywhere in the country with unlimited minutes on nights and weekends.

THE END. ☺

Kaley,

Wow. Did you read the assigned chapters thoroughly? It sounds as if you merely skimmed them.

Please read more carefully.

Mr. Serrano

September 20
World History
Unit: Writing Essays
Grade 4
Mr. Serrano

People: The Later Years
by Kaley Bluster

For anyone who thinks I did not read
the assigned chapters thoroughly, information about the next age can be found
on pages 38 to 45 in <u>The World:
Past, Present, and Future</u>, Moody,
Green, & Fink Publishers, New York,
London, Toronto, Sidney, copyright 2003.

The next age was called the New Stone
Age because everybody had gotten so used

to saying, "Hey, it's the Stone Age," that they couldn't think of anything better to call it.

Suddenly the earth wasn't as cold anymore. People started taking off their jackets and running around in togas.

The ice melted, and guess what people discovered beneath it? Farms! Now they could quit wandering all over creation following those smelly mammoths, stay home, and eat veggies.

The kids weren't crazy about this plan, so they encouraged their parents to "domesticate" animals. That meant they could have meat and milk with their vegetables. Sadly, a long time would pass

before someone figured out how
to invent pizza and Pepsi.

Now that people weren't moving
around all the time, civilizations sprang up.
I'm not sure how a civilization can "spring,"
but that's the exact wording in the text,
page 41, paragraph 3, of the chapter I am
reading thoroughly.

It was time for people to settle down
and elect a government. The government
immediately made up a bunch of rules
telling people what they could and couldn't
do—sort of like school. This was considered
a dark period in history.

During the New Stone Age, many villages also "sprang up," mostly along rivers.

This way, people had water for drinking, for washing dishes and clothes, and for taking baths. All in all, it doesn't sound very sanitary. This would not bother my stinky cousin, Cal, at all.

Hunting and gathering was no longer necessary, which was okay with everyone who'd grown tired of the squabbling. Now people began to specialize in various skills.

Some made pottery, others made baskets, and some designed jewelry. One person opened the first yoga studio (like my mom!), but she was way ahead of her time, and it just didn't catch on.

THE END. ☺

Kaley,

Please see me after school.

Mr. Serrano

September 25
World History
Unit: Writing Essays
Grade 4
Mr. Serrano

Advanced Civilizations
by Kaley Bluster

A truly advanced, civilized person would never make a student stay after school to make sure she "understood the reading assignment," especially when that student's mother had gone to the hospital to give birth to a baby sister.

baby sister

I found this out when Aunt Phoebe came to pick up Cal and me after school, in case anyone reading this is interested.

When Aunt Phoebe was told that I was being "detained," Cal whispered, "It serves you right." How could he say that? He doesn't even know why I'm staying late. He's lucky I missed when I swung.

So here I am in row two, seat four. I will stay and write this account because my future baby sister will need to learn stuff like this when she is older, and better she learns it from me.

About Civilizations:

Sooner or later, one was bound to zoom ahead of the others. Civilizations are like that. This happened in the Nile River Valley to a bunch of really smart people.

The Nile River is in Egypt, which is mostly desert. People had to figure out how to irrigate crops by building canals. This was a very advanced idea for the times and earned them two full pages (54-55) of <u>The World: Past, Present, and Future</u>. (In case anyone is checking.)

An important city in the Nile Valley was called Memphis. Everyone knows that this is where Elvis got his start. My Grandmother Bluster is crazy about Elvis, even though he is dead. She has a picture of him inside a little drawer on her nightstand. Don't ask how I know this, because it makes me sound snoopy.

In Memphis, there was a great palace where the Egyptian Pharaoh, King Menes, lived. I think the palace was called Graceland.

The Nile Valley is where the Great Pyramids were built. The tallest pyramid is as high as a 48-story building. These were built as tombs for dead pharaohs. Boy, did they have ego problems.

Some of the structures took 100,000 workers 20 years to build. Sadly, they had no pizza or Pepsi to sustain them in the blazing desert sun.

People of today wonder how the Egyptians built the pyramids without modern tools and trucks. I don't know the answer to this, even though I read the paragraph about it on page 59 <u>FIVE</u> times.

To find the answer, you'll have to use an "alternative source," which is what Ms. Bartholomew in the library is teaching us to do.

Ms. Bart is very helpful. (Pretty, too, if you like red hair.) Her dog had puppies and she is trying to find a good home for the last one, which might be of interest to anyone reading this who has too much time on his hands for grading papers when he could be out walking his new dog.

Near the biggest pyramid of all sits the Sphinx. It's a lion with a human head, built to scare away tourists so they won't leave soda cans on the steps of the crumbling pyramids.

For years, the Sphinx was the largest carved head in the world—until four presidents' faces were carved on the side of Mount Rushmore in South Dakota.

Our leaders do not have egos as big as the pharaohs because no dead presidents are buried beneath Mount Rushmore. At least none that I know of.

In 1922, an archaeologist discovered the tomb of a pharaoh named King Tutankhamen. No one knew how to spell or pronounce his name, so they nicknamed him King Tut.

His tomb was an amazing maze of underground hallways and hidden rooms with secret entrances. Cal and I would love it because it sounds like a really cool place to play—except for the fact there's a dead person inside.

King Tut was crowned when he was only nine years old. He ruled Egypt his entire life and died at the ripe old age of nineteen. Some say he died trying to learn how to spell his name.

THE END. ☺

Kaley,

You have an interesting way of interpreting history. Or rather, <u>twisting</u> history.

Enough about civilizations. Since you seem to enjoy creative writing (even though the assignment clearly asked for essays—which use FACTS), give me a brief discourse on early forms of writing.

I did not know you were expecting a little sister. Congrats!

I thought Ms. Bartholomew had found a home for all the pups.

                    Mr. Serrano

October 2nd
World History
Unit: Writing Essays
Grade 4
Mr. Serrano

Early Writing
by Kaley Bluster

First of all, I don't know what a "discourse" is.

Second of all, this essay was really hard to write because I had to use Ms. Bart's "alternative sources," which means I've stayed after school in the library two afternoons in a row.

The good part is that I got to search online, which was fun. Ms. Bartholomew showed me how. She couldn't believe any teacher would be mean enough to give me an extra essay to write in addition to the assigned topics.

Third of all, I am not happy.

My mom finally had her baby last night.

Guess what? It's a BOY!!!

This will never do because I've already made lots of plans for my new baby sister and me. Girl things, like playing movie star. I cannot play movie star with a brother.

Cal told me the baby would be just like him. Triple ewww!

Fourth of all, Ms. Bart <u>does</u> have one last puppy, and she is <u>desperate</u> to find a home for him.

I want him! But my mom insists that one new baby in the house is enough. (Even though she knows I'd rather have a puppy than a <u>brother</u>.)

I told Ms. Bart you might be interested in getting a dog.

And now I have to think about "early forms of writing," which, in spite of the extra time it took to research, is a very interesting topic because that is what I want to be when I grow up.

I know a lot about writing because my Uncle Anthony (Cal's father) is a journalist who has written a book, and he keeps me informed.

All about writing:

Long before e-mail, one of the greatest advances in ancient history was the development of writing. The earliest examples of writing used pictures called "hieroglyphics."

Oddly enough, the word "hieroglyphics" is completely impossible to illustrate. You think they would've called this type of writing "cat" or something easier to draw.

People used to write on "papyrus," a

paper made from reeds. They flattened and glued sheets of papyrus together to make scrolls.

They made ink out of soot from the fire and wrote with pens made—again—from reeds. Apparently reeds were very important in those days. Nowadays, you hardly see one.

People who knew how to write were called scribes. At first, everyone wanted to call them reeds, but someone decided that was overkill.

Scribes kept important records for the pharaohs. Since they were the only ones who could read and write, they were treated with great respect and kindness. This is not true of writers today, according to Uncle Anthony, whose book has been rejected fourteen times.

Hundreds of years after the time of scribes and pharaohs, no one had a clue what the hieroglyphics meant. No one, that is, until someone discovered the Rosetta Stone.

The Rosetta Stone is a large, black rock with the same message carved in three languages. Besides hieroglyphics, the words were also written in Egyptian and Greek, which everybody knew. Well, not everybody—just the Egyptians and the Greeks.

Because of the Rosetta Stone, people were able to interpret hieroglyphics and figure out what all the squiggly pictures meant.

About the same time, down the road in Sumeria, another type of writing called "cuneiform" was invented. Sumerian scribes wrote on clay tablets with a stylus made out of—surprise!—a reed.

People in Sumeria believed that a writer had "magical powers" over a person or an object because he could write its name. For this reason, writers here were also treated with honor.

Me—
with
magical
powers

I told Uncle Anthony about this and he said, "Boy, how times have changed."

As for me, I like the idea of a writer having magical powers.

THE END. ☺

Kaley,

This is better, but I still think you need to stick to the FACTS and not embellish them.

Congratulations on the new baby brother! What's his name?

I have read your uncle's articles in the newspaper, but did not know he'd written a novel. What is the title?

I'm not interested in getting a dog, but thanks for thinking of me.

Mr. Serrano

October 10
World History
Unit: Writing Essays
Grade 4
Mr. Serrano

Assignment #2:
Discuss and compare the
Greek and Roman Empires.

The Greek Empire
by Kaley Bluster

FACT: My brother's name is Matthew
Alexander Bluster.

FACT: My uncle's book has now been
rejected <u>fifteen</u> times.

FACT: His book is called <u>How to Write a
Novel and Get it Published</u>.

What does "embellish the FACTS" mean?

Ms. Bart is bringing King to school tomorrow so you can meet him. I named him!  (After King Menes of Egypt.) I figure he needs a BIG name because he is a very small puppy.

About the Greeks:

Today's world owes much to the Greeks and their contributions to art and literature. They believed in many different gods, who each had a job.

Poseidon was the god of the sea, and Aphrodite was the goddess of love. Zeus was in charge of the weather. In my opinion,

Zeus hasn't been doing a very good job lately and should get his act together.

A famous Greek poet was named Homer. His last name was not Simpson. He wrote two epic poems about the war between the Greeks and the Trojans. They were called <u>The Iliad</u> and <u>The Odyssey</u>.

I don't know anyone who's read them, but I heard it's required when you get to high school. I think you get extra credit if you understand them.

In the United States, our systems of democracy and trial by jury are based on early ideas from Athens, the capital of Greece. Even though Washington and

Jefferson and those other guys who wrote the Constitution make you think these things were their ideas, the Greeks really thought of them first. So there.

One of the greatest gifts Greece gave to us was the Olympics. The first Olympic Games were held in 776 B.C. I'm not sure which network covered it. The 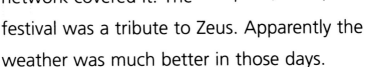 festival was a tribute to Zeus. Apparently the weather was much better in those days.

In the early Olympic Games, women were not allowed to compete. They were not even allowed to WATCH. What was that all about?

Also, there was only
one event—a foot race. The
winner didn't receive a gold
medal. He received a crown of olive leaves.
Ho hum.

Cal told me that the first Olympic run-
ners ran naked. I do not believe this, but he
says it's a FACT. Maybe that's why they
didn't let the girls watch.

Greece also gave us the theater.
Dionysus ruled over the festivals of plays. He
was the god of pleasure. If a play was really
awful, he let Zeus take over for the night so
he didn't get blamed. People were usually
mad at Zeus anyway, especially if it rained in
the middle of Act One.

One playwright, Aeschylus (don't ask me how to pronounce it) was known as the "father of tragedy" because he wrote sad plays. Aristophanes (ditto) wrote funny plays and became the "father of comedy."

If they were alive today, they'd probably be writing TV shows. But not together because one was funny and one was serious. And if they wanted to succeed in Hollywood, they'd have to change their names to something easier to pronounce on "Entertainment Tonight."

The most famous Greek of all was

Socrates. He was a philosopher, which means he sat around and thought a lot. Apparently, he thought too much, because the government sentenced him to death for getting people to question Athens's customs, laws, and values.

While he was in jail, someone gave him a cup of hemlock. If Socrates was really so smart, how could he drink a whole cup of poison? Triple ewww!

About the Romans:

Rome wasn't built in a day. It took centuries. And centurions (Roman generals). The legend of the birth of Rome is kind of hard to swallow, but I, a writer-to-be, love stories, so here goes:

A princess gave birth to twin boys and named them Romulus and Remus. Their uncle wanted the throne for himself without a couple of cute baby nephews breathing down his neck. (I can relate to the baby part.)

The cruel uncle packed the twins into a basket and sailed them down the Tiber River to drown. (No, I would not do this to baby Matthew, but I might do it to Cal, who has already taught Matthew how to burp.)

As in all good fairy tales, the babies

were rescued by a wolf, who took them to her den and raised them with her cubs. (I warned you the story was hard to swallow.)

Soon, a kindly shepherd adopted the boys. After they grew up to be young men, they drove their cruel uncle from the throne and declared Romulus king. Romulus built the city of Rome on the spot where he and his brother had been rescued by the wolf.

The cruel uncle went off to work in a Roman chariot factory, and the wolf got a job in another fairy tale. (Okay, I made that part up.)

From 500 B.C. on, the city of Rome grew into a vast empire that included most of the known world. How did they do it?

Foot soldiers.

The soldiers were part of a large and powerful army with all the latest weapons: Rock throwers! Flaming arrows! A tower of stairs!

Yes, stairs helped the Romans win many a battle. A tall tower was built on wheels and rolled up to the walls of an enemy city. Soldiers hustled up the steps and walked right over the walls to conquer one and all.

I think this type of fighting became known as Stair Wars.

Comparisons:

The Greeks gave us the Olympics and theater, so the Romans (not to be outdone) also gave things of importance to the world.

The Romans built an amazing bunch of roads that connected the empire. The roads were built so well that some are still around today.

Hard to believe you could walk down a road that's over 2,000 years old. As my grandfather says (the one who is married to the grandma who loves Elvis): "They don't make things like they used to."

The Romans are also famous for their "aqueducts," a system of tunnels built through mountains and across valleys to supply water to cities. I think the aqueducts were designed by a Roman named Caesar Plumber. His designs are still around today.

One of the Romans' greatest accomplishments was the Coliseum, a huge sports arena with four stories of marble seats, columns, arches, and daily shows.

The bad part was that shows were fights to the death between gladiators. Or between wild animals and slaves, prisoners of war, or followers of a brand-new religion called Christianity.

The battles were very scary, and the animals usually won. I think the Romans had a strange way of having fun.

As my grandfather also says, "All good things come to an end." But how did this gigantic empire decline? Did the Romans get too big for their togas?

Here's what happened. After a time of peace and prosperity, 25 new emperors were murdered in only 50 short years. (Note: This is a FACT that surely would have made it into the Guinness Book of World Records if the book had been around in those days.)

Next came Barbarians from the north, tramping all over the empire and sacking cities. Suddenly all of the rules changed. Or, long story short, the Roman Empire fell and nobody was there to catch it.

The end of ancient times. ☺

Kaley,

Thank you for weaving a few
FACTS into your report. I don't
think you are a "writer-to-be."
I think you are a writer _now_.

Baby brothers aren't so bad. I
had two of them and only got beat
up a few times. (I'm kidding.)
We are friends today.

Well, okay, I'll have a look at the
pup in the library, since you went to
all the trouble to pick a good name
for him. But I'm _really_ not looking
for a pet.

                    Mr. Serrano

October 17
World History
Unit: Writing Essays
Grade 4
Mr. Serrano

Assignment #3: Discuss the Middle Ages.

Include references to monasteries, the Crusades, and the Renaissance.

Use one example each: a graph, a chart, a footnote, a map.

The Middle Ages
by Kaley Bluster

When people hear the term "Middle Ages," they usually think of grown-ups in their thirties. (No offense, Mr. S.) In this case, I am talking about a period of history that falls between ancient and modern times.

The Middle Ages began in the 6th century. Today, we live in the 21st century. To give you an idea how long ago that was, I will use a <u>chart</u> since that is one of the requirements of this assignment:

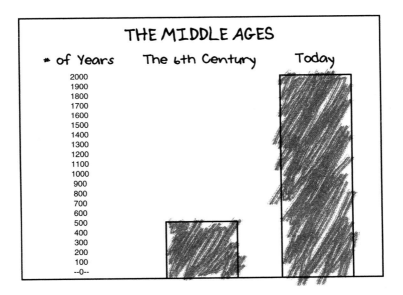

THE MIDDLE AGES

# of Years   The 6th Century   Today

2000
1900
1800
1700
1600
1500
1400
1300
1200
1100
1000
900
800
700
600
500
400
300
200
100
--0--

In the 6th century, a group of people lived in northern Europe. Everyone had the same name: Frank. For this reason, we call their civilization "The Franks."

The Franks had a bad habit of wandering off to visit neighboring villages, then not going home until they'd raided and plundered and conquered the town.

(Note: never invite a Frank to your birthday party.)

After 200 years, most of Europe was filled with Franks. It was time to elect a ruler. They chose Charlemagne (a.k.a. "Charles the Great"). Historians believe they chose him because his mother (Frank) dared to give him a different name.

This was a brilliant move on her part. When it was time for the elections, here is what the ballot looked like:

VOTE FOR ONE:

Frank ☐
Frank ☐
Frank ☐
Frank ☐
Charles ☐
Frank ☐
Frank ☐
Frank ☐
Frank ☐

No wonder he won.

After that, the idea of using a different name caught on like those crazy Roman sandals, and, for a while, all new babies were named Charles.

Still, traces of Franks remain to this day. For example, my grandfather's name is Frank (not Elvis, as much as my grandma would like that).

Charlemagne turned out to be a great ruler. During his rule, he conquered most of Europe. He might have gone on to conquer the rest of the world, but nobody knew it was there yet.

As all great rulers do, Charlemagne died. Immediately, Northmen (men from the

North) sailed from Scandinavia and began raiding villages in Europe.

Boy, was it payback time. Now the Franks got a big taste of their own medicine.

These Northmen were the Vikings. For the next 250 years, they ran around Europe in the dark, surprising people and stealing goats and land.

Kings were so afraid of Vikings that they paid noblemen to protect them while they holed up in their castles. Castles were cold, dark, and dusty because nobody had invented furnaces, lamps, or vacuum cleaners yet. Or bathrooms.

What if nature called in the middle of the night, and you tip-toed outside and ran smack into a Viking snooping around the castle wall? Scary!

outhouse

Cal is going to be a Viking for Halloween. In case you were wondering how he knows about them, he is in the other 4th grade class (mean Mrs. Fritz's), and they are studying the Vikings, too.

(I probably shouldn't call Mrs. Fritz "mean," but anyone reading this knows she won't allow talking AT ALL and gives homework on Fridays. I am glad we write our essays during study time.)

I am also glad Cal is in <u>her</u> class. It serves him right.

For Halloween, I am going to be an ancient Egyptian because I love the pictures of them on pages 65-66. Grandma Bluster made me a tunic decorated with Egyptian designs to wear over my jeans because my mother is so busy with that baby she doesn't have time to make a costume for her only daughter.

My mother <u>did</u> promise to let me use her eye makeup as part of my costume, so I guess she is helping a little.

Back to the Middle Ages!!

Surrounding the castles were farming estates called manors. There were good manors and bad manors, and everyone was expected to know the difference by the age of five.

It was important for manors to be self-sufficient. This kept people close to home. No one ordered out for pizza in those days. What if the delivery boy was a Viking in disguise?

Everything they needed was made on manor grounds. If you got a craving for something fancy, like Spam, you pretty much had to face the fact you were born fifteen centuries too soon. (Note: refer to required chart, seven pages back.)

Eventually, the Vikings decided they could make more friends than enemies if they traded instead of raided, so off they went to explore other lands, hoping to bring back some really cool stuff to trade.

Lucky for everyone, the Vikings returned from faraway lands, politely ringing doorbells this time instead of stealing chickens and setting fire to huts.

They traded gems, cloth, and spices from other lands for pigs, gold, and such.

Centuries later, the Vikings' idea of selling things door-to-door was adopted by today's Girl Scouts, of which I am a member, not to mention the FACT that I am very good at selling cookies door to door.

Here is a <u>graph</u> to show you how good I am:

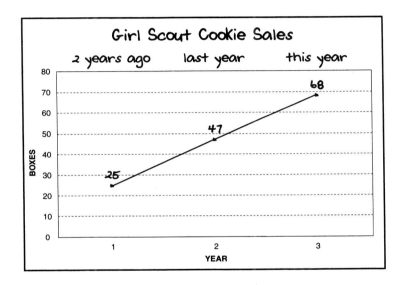

I was hoping to hand down my uniform to my baby sister, but forget it. I don't think Matthew will want to be a Girl Scout.

Castles:

(Which we weren't asked to discuss, but were very important in the Middle Ages, which is why I keep talking about them. Plus, I <u>looooove</u> castles and like to think about living in one.)

Everyone knows the story of Cinderella. (Cal says he doesn't, but he is either teasing or stupid. Probably both.)

There is a king, a queen, a handsome prince. A lavish ball. A shoe. And the beautiful princess, of course.

I wish I could be a princess growing up in a castle. It sounds like a pretty cushy life with gowns, jewels, servants, and ladies-in-waiting at your beck and call.

Since I don't want to "embellish the FACTS," I will note that the textbook says most medieval kids lived in small huts on the manor grounds. No rooms of their own, no computer, PlayStation, or instant-messaging with friends. Instead, the entire family slept in one bed to keep warm. Weird!

In the mornings, moms didn't pester kids to take a shower and put on clean underwear because they believed bathing caused diseases.

Most bathed only a few times a year. Try that today and see what happens.

(I would draw a graph to show you how many showers Cal takes in a month, but the graph would be very small and I've already fulfilled my graph-making obligation for this assignment.)

On the castle grounds, the father might work as a blacksmith shoeing horses, a miller grinding wheat, a baker, or a gardener.

A mother would <u>not</u> be a yoga instructor like mine. Or at least she was before the baby came. Now she complains about never fitting into her yoga pants again.

Instead, a mother would spend all her time preparing food, sewing clothes, and making towels and bedding. How would your mom feel about making bedspreads from scratch? I'm afraid to ask mine. She won't even use a diaper unless she can throw it away.

In those days, there were no grocery stores. People sold food and other stuff from the windows of their huts.

A mom might buy flour for bread from a miller, fruit from a farmer, or needles and thread from a tailor. She probably wouldn't enjoy shopping because everyone threw garbage into the streets.

Between the garbage and the people who didn't believe in bathing, it was necessary to hold a bouquet of flowers or herbs to your nose so the smell wouldn't kill you. Or at least carry around a bottle of Febreze.

Boys became apprentices to their fathers or to other merchants on the manor. Or even at a manor far away. Imagine moving out at the age of seven.

Girls would likely do the same. I am considering it since I am not getting any sleep because somebody cries and fusses ALL NIGHT LONG.

The problem with girls becoming apprentices is that the only job they were trained to do was run a household. Yawn. They worked from sunup to sundown without "Oprah" to watch while ironing. (They didn't even <u>have</u> irons.) They never took vacations, and I don't think they were even allowed to have headaches, which my mother has been having a lot of lately.

If you were the son of the manor lord, you would learn how to read and write, but only in Latin. Girls were not taught. (I hope Cal isn't paying attention in Mrs. Fritz's class, because knowing this will make him more obnoxious.)

Boys also trained for knighthood. So at the age of nine, off you'd go to live in another castle. First you'd become a page (a messenger), and then at fourteen, you'd become a squire. This meant you would serve one of the castle's knights, taking care of his horse, polishing his armor, and answering his chain mail. (← This is a joke, Mr. S., not a FACT.)

You would learn how to fight with a sword and lance—which is nothing more than a long, pointed stick. If your own personal knight rode off to war, you'd ride along with him without having to ask your parents for permission.

If you managed to stay alive, you'd kneel before the king and become a knight yourself. Then you could have your own squire, your own pointed stick, and a lot of battles in your future.

I would like to get me one of those

pointed sticks. Maybe I could ask for one
for my birthday, which is in a few days but
which will probably be forgotten by a
mother who is constantly coo-coo-cooing
that baby.

Monasteries:

(Which we <u>do</u> have to mention.)

A thousand years ago, religious
leaders built hundreds of monasteries for
boys who became monks, and convents for
girls who became nuns.

These were similar to kingdoms because
they were self-sufficient, too. But
monasteries had something castles did not.
Libraries.

That's the good news.

The bad news is that all the books were written by hand. If you wanted a copy, you had to write the book all over again.

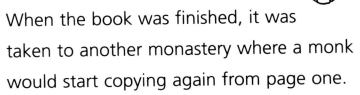

When the book was finished, it was taken to another monastery where a monk would start copying again from page one.

I guess we should be thankful there were no TVs, online surfing, or video games to distract the monks. If they hadn't copied information about the Greeks and Romans, we wouldn't have to suffer through writing essays about them 1500 years later.

(Speaking of online surfing, it might be of interest to know that my Uncle

Anthony has decided to publish his book himself. It will be posted on his Web site: www.how2getpubbed.com.)

With all these monasteries, convents, and cathedrals popping up all over, you can imagine that this was a time of great religious "fervor." (← From the text, so it must be correct, although I don't know this word.)

People thought nothing of taking off on a pilgrimage to the Holy Land. (These are the Crusades, which I am also supposed to mention.)

"Pilgrimage" means "walking to a holy place." We're talking hundreds of miles. How did they know the way? They traveled east until they stepped in Greece, then followed the shoreline until they hit the Red Sea.

Here is a <u>map</u> to show you the path to the Holy Land during the Crusades, thus fulfilling the map part of my assignment:

One trip to the Holy Land turned out badly. The Turks (people from Turkey) decided they didn't want the Christians to come, so when they arrived, the Turks killed them.

How rude! Couldn't they simply have posted signs along the way asking the Christians to go home?

Turn back NOW!!

We're Serious

This riled up a lot of people in Europe, so they sent crusaders off to the Holy Lands to squash the Turks. Everybody went—kings and queens, nuns and monks, serfs and noblemen.

This means You!

STOP!

But once they got there, they forgot all about capturing the Holy Land because they discovered things that were just as important. Cinnamon! Oranges! Rice! And lots of other stuff they'd never tasted before.

They stocked up and returned to Europe, hoping the folks back home would over-look the failed Crusades as long as they could now have lemon in their tea and pepper on their eggs.

It worked.

Now people started running back and forth between Europe and the Middle East so often, those old Roman roads had to be spruced up.

Not only that, but folks began stopping at crossroads to buy and sell all the great stuff people from other lands wanted to buy. The crossroads soon became villages, which grew into towns, which grew into cities.

CROSS RD

Everyone began to leave the castles and manors and move to the cities for a brand-new way of life. Raiding was forgotten, and kings became an endangered species.

Here is a little <u>chart</u> for extra credit since I already drew one earlier:

IN	TEN MINUTES AGO	OUT
city life	kingdoms	raiding and plundering

Kings did not like losing power over their domains, so they put impossible taxes on people in order to continue their lives of luxury.

Noblemen rebelled by writing up a list of freedoms. The kings knew if they didn't sign the agreement, their subjects would rise up against them.

This list of rights was called the Magna Carta. I think it sounds a lot like our Declaration of Independence.

If all these history assignments keep coming, I'm going to write up my own Magna Carta. Let me know if it works.

On to the Renaissance!

(which happens to be a very hard word
to spell)

The miserable Crusades were over,
cities were springing up across Europe, and
business was booming for merchants.

But something was missing.

People wanted to bring back the
great literature, art, and ideas that made
the Romans and Greeks famous.

Sort of like a comeback tour in the known
world.

Interest in old art inspired
new art. Interest in old literature
and previous ideas inspired new
literature and fresh ideas.

This time of rebirth was called the Renaissance. It seemed as if Europe drank a giant mug of double latte espresso and suddenly woke up from the Dark Ages after a long winter's nap.

This was a time of great creativity and progress—not unlike the last five minutes before it's time to turn in one of our history essays.

Everyone has heard of Michelangelo, the famous artist with only one name. Artistic types are hip like that.

Michelangelo was the guy who lay on his back to paint the ceiling of the Sistine Chapel in Rome.

He also wrote poetry and made sculptures from blocks of marble. He believed human shapes were already formed inside the marble, waiting for him to free them.

I wish my essays were finished inside one of the class computers and all I had to do was free them from the monitor.

Leonardo DaVinci was another famous artist during the Renaissance. He was creative, too, although he had two names—three if you count the "Da."

His most famous painting was the "Mona Lisa." (Two first names!)

famous
Smile

Leo was a doodler, like me. He drew pictures in more than 5,000 notebooks. It must have driven his teachers crazy.

Some of the stuff he came up with was way ahead of its time. Like an airplane—hundreds of years before one was invented.

He also drew very detailed sketches of human muscles and bones. How did he know what they looked like? He cut people open and looked!!! Dead people, of course, but still—triple ewww!

(Note: if anyone named Leo offers to sketch a picture of you, RUN!)

A hundred years later, something happened that changed the world forever. A man invented a machine that could copy books. You might think his name was Kinko, but no—it was Gutenberg.

Gutenberg's press could print a page in minutes. This was great news for those poor monks, suffering from carpal tunnel syndrome after copying all those pages in fancy letters.

Having more books published faster meant more information was going out into the world, and more people were learning how to read. An explosion of learning followed, which led to the founding of public libraries.

This was immediately followed by the invention of the library fine for overdue books. Only in those days,  you could pay your fine with a basket of eggs or a head of cabbage. Please do not try this today.

Thus ends the Middle Ages and this assignment. (◄ That's how they talked in those days.)

Ooops, I forgot to include a footnote.[1]

---

[1] This is what it looks like.

Kaley,

You certainly make the Dark Ages sound more interesting than they probably were.

However, I must take off points because your graph pertains to personal data, not historical facts. And your footnote does not give me additional information.

I will give you extra credit for the second chart; however, it is more correctly referred to as a "table."

Did you really sell that many boxes of Girl Scout cookies?

                              Mr. Serrano

P.S. Happy birthday!

November 3rd
World History
Unit: Writing Essays
Grade 4
Mr. Serrano

Assignment #3: Modern Times
Students will draw a topic card from
each category:

1. Man's Greatest Inventions
2. Social Services That Influenced
   the 20th Century

Topic Card #1: The Airplane

I do not like losing points

because directions were not clear.[1]

foot note

---

[1] Directions stated: Use an example of a graph. Further details were
not provided.

Actual number of Girl Scout cookie boxes sold minus two that Cal ate and I had to pay for since he had no money.[2]

About this topic: For my birthday[3] I received a book called <u>Famous Women Inventors</u>.[4]

Therefore, I feel that the topic "Man's Greatest Inventions" implies that women invented nothing, which is not true, according to the book. Therefore, I will write this essay from the woman's point of view.

---

[2] 66

[3] November 1st. And yes, my baby-obsessed mother remembered and gave me a party. The cake was not homemade, but I can be forgiving if the chocolate frosting is thick enough.

[4] Grandma Bluster is big on educational books and toys.

The Airplane
by Kaley Bluster

Not much has been written about Sadie and Eliza ("The Brain") Wright. These two, also known as the Wright Sisters, had barely tiptoed into the 20th century when they were picnicking on the bank of a stream near their home in North Carolina.

A noise in the bushes sent a cloud of starlings into the air and across the clear blue sky.

"I wish I could fly like that," Sadie is reported to have said. (Dreamily.)

"Why not try?" Eliza is reported to have replied. (Determinedly.)

That is why everyone called Eliza "The Brain," because she always said "yes" whenever seemingly impossible tasks were set before her.

Like the time she borrowed her brother Orville's pants and boots to go riding because she thought it silly to wear a dress and sit sideways on a pony. To this day, girls wear pants to ride and rarely sit sideways.

The Wright sisters gathered their picnic supplies and hurried home. There, they found Orville with their other brother Wilbur making mechanical toys to sell.

Sadie picked up a toy glider and sailed it across the room. "Let's make one of these people-sized!" she exclaimed. "So we can fly across the sky like starlings."

Just to humor her, the boys set to work with their tools. Meanwhile, Eliza read all she could find on aeronautics, which was not a whole lot in those days.

She hung out with her brothers as they worked, telling them how long the wings should be, how to angle them against the wind, and how to calculate air pressure.

Sadie designed a seat so a person could sit comfortably while steering (in a dress or pants). When she was finished, she built a lightweight engine (with the help of Eliza's brain).

Soon it was time for Sadie and Eliza to test their flying machine. They scouted a good location, choosing a nearby hill outside of Kitty Hawk.

On the big day, the four carted their aircraft to Kill Devil Hill. At the last minute, Sadie had second thoughts about the safety of the whole thing and wished she'd designed crash helmets. Eliza was worried, too. She wasn't absolutely sure her calculations had been correct.

On top of that, they were both wearing new velvet dresses with lace flounces— which were all the rage in 1903.

So, like any good sisters, they decided to stay safe and clean on a wool blanket on the grass while their totally-boy-brothers did the daredevil deed, flying off the hill instead of them.

And, hey, it worked! Four flights. The longest one was 59 seconds.

Newspaper reporters were waiting when the boys landed, and, in all the excitement, they gave the Wright brothers every bit of credit for the flight. Therefore, the boys ended up in the history books instead of their sisters.

Sadie and Eliza really didn't mind. They were much too busy making sketches for a new talking device they were inventing for their old friend, Alex G. Bell.

THE END. ☺

Kaley,

All I can say is that you're
definitely getting an A in
creative writing.

        Mr. Serrano,
        considering
        early retirement

November 10th

Kaley,

You are late turning in your essay for Topic Card 2-Social Services That Influenced the 20th Century.

According to my records, you picked "History of Medicine."

You are never late with assignments. Do you need help? Extra time?

Please feel free to ask me or Ms. Bart for help.

By the way, I met King. He is going to _need_ a big name like that because he's definitely the runt of the litter.

Mr. Serrano

November 11
World History
Unit: Writing Essays
Grade 4
Mr. Serrano

Topic Card #2
Discuss the following social service:
The History of Medicine.

Medicine
by Kaley Bluster

Medicine was very important to the
20th century. Many new pills were invented.
Doctors learned how to operate
on people. Hospitals were built.
Some people, like my Grandma
Bluster, started volunteering in gift shops at

hospitals along with other grandmas and grandpas.

THE END. ☺

P.S. Well? What did you think of the puppy?

Kaley,

I want to talk to you after school.

Mr. Serrano

November 14th

Kaley,

I'm glad we talked on Friday afternoon.

I am sorry your baby brother has been sick, and that your mother had to spend the whole weekend at the hospital with him.

Your grandmother is keeping me posted. Meanwhile, I am sending some books for you home with Cal. "Mean" Mrs. Fritz said it was okay.

Don't worry about your final essay on Topic Card #2. Write it when you return to class.

Would it make you feel better to know that King now has a home? Yes, I adopted him. He is doing fine and has only eaten two pairs of my shoes. Heaven help me!

Mr. Serrano

P.S. Thank you for not naming the puppy Tutankhamen.

November 17
World History
Unit: Writing Essays
Grade 4
Mr. Serrano

Topic Card #2: DO OVER

History of Medicine
by Kaley Bluster

Don't worry, this essay won't be as boring as it sounds.

I feel like an expert on medicine after a week of sitting in the pediatric waiting room in the Our Lady of Fatima wing of the St. Something or Other Hospital. (I remember the Lady's name because she gazed down on me no matter where I sat in the waiting room.)

Sometimes Aunt Phoebe sat with me, sometimes Grandpa Bluster, and sometimes Cal, who behaved himself because Our Lady was watching.

I am sorry for all the bad things I said about baby Matthew. He has been in an incubator for days, hooked up to lots of tubes. He looked very small and miserable when the doctor let me have a peek at him. I wondered if he was afraid.

He is going to be okay, now that they have his infection under control. I never saw my mother cry before. It scared me.

Thank you for sending the books. How did you know I like stories about castles?

Are you really meeting Ms. Bart for coffee after school to talk about the care and feeding of puppies? That's what she told me when I checked out <u>Medicine through the Ages</u>.

I feel up to writing my essay now, so here goes:

Earlier, I wrote about people in the Stone Age. What did they do when they got sick? Well, first of all, they only lived to be 25 or 30, so they didn't have a whole lot of years for aching and paining. Causes of death ranged from a common cold to being run over by a stampeding herd of mammoths.

Nowadays, no one ever dies from

stampeding mammoths, yet scientists are still working on a cure for the common cold.

As time progressed, people began to notice that when they ate certain leaves or roots, it often improved their health. For example, one night after feasting on way more raw antelope than a person should, a boy named Klug (not his real name) chewed on a few peppermint leaves. In a surprising turn of events, his bellyache instantly improved.

Encouraged, Klug scouted the forest, looking for "earth foods" to make himself taller, clear his sinuses, and attract a pretty girl down by the Lwap River. Her name was Klig (not her real name).

Sadly, Klug never found a root to make himself taller, but he did discover that blackberries improved his stuffy nose. And rubbing rose petals behind his ears did the trick with Klig. (A bath helped, too.)

The children and grandchildren of Klug and Klig continued to experiment with flowers, leaves, and stems, and they passed this knowledge on to future generations.

By the age of the Egyptians (remember them?) thousands of uses for herbal remedies had been recorded.

In the Middle Ages, the practice of

healing with natural remedies blossomed. Often, a village woman would become an expert on teas and potions for every ailment. Some villages called these ladies "wise women" and others called them "witches." They believed the potions were magic. And, in a way, they were.

If you were suffering from a pounding headache and the village wise woman brewed tea from feverfew leaves and the tea made your headache disappear, wouldn't you think it was magic, too?

In 1900, there were very few doctors since folks still knew and used many home remedies. Here are a few:

1. Put honey on a bee sting. It's a natural antiseptic.

2. Drink wild cherry tea for coughs. (That is why you see wild cherry flavored cough drops.)

3. Eat garlic if you have an infection. It's "nature's antibiotic."

4. Put clove oil on a toothache.

5. For a stomachache, sip peppermint tea, like Klug, or take ginger. (That is why your mother brings you ginger ale when your tummy hurts.)

   People seemed to be healthier back then, too. Cancer was rare, and the first heart attack wasn't recorded in medical journals until the early 1900s.

Then came 1928 and the discovery of penicillin. This began the modern age of medicine. Suddenly, natural cures were old-fashioned. Doctors pooh-poohed them—even though they worked.

No one thought to question this because pills became all the rage. Pills for the heart, liver, head, and stomach. Pills for every ailment. No more teas  or compresses or chewing on roots and leaves.

Some of the natural cures were even turned into pills. Today's aspirin is made from a substance found in white willow bark. A heart pill called "digitalis" is made from a plant called foxglove.

But the best part of all is that pills cost money. Lots of money. Roots and leaves were free, but nobody was making money watching people get well the natural way.

For the next few decades, pills ruled. At the same time, cancer and heart disease became the leading causes of death.

It seemed like medicine was going backward instead of forward. In the 1990s, people started noticing that all the medical advances were not making people healthier.

Some returned to the idea of drinking queen-of-the-meadow tea to dissolve gallstones instead of having their gall bladder removed. Some started sipping elderberry juice to get over the flu.

They discovered something else about natural cures. Food is the best medicine.

I don't think anyone wants to eat raw antelope like Klug, but folks who eat roots (like carrots, beets, and onions), leaves (salads), and stems (celery and asparagus) may not have as many health problems as those who fill up on Meatos, Furridos, Mice Cream, and Tepsi (not their real names).

Perhaps those Stone Age root chewers had the right idea, and today's pill makers should take a lesson from history—even if they don't make as much money.

Meanwhile, my brother gets to come home from the hospital tomorrow. I'm going to be nicer to him. Maybe I'll be nicer to Cal, too. After all, he went to the gift shop at the hospital and spent his allowance on a box of tissues so I could cry.

He's not a bad cousin.

Some of the time.

THE END. ☺

Kaley,

Welcome back to class.
We missed you.

About your final essay: In
between all the fiction, you gave
us a lot of very interesting FACTS.
Good job.

World History Unit on
Writing Essays: A

Following instructions: C

                    Mr. Serrano

P.S. Never change.